10 Not So Interesting Facts ABOUT CACTUS

(That I may or may not have made up...)

A PASSWORD BOOK IN CAMOUFLAGE

JESSICA R. HERRERA

Characactus: Frond Fieldstone

Cactus Facts

(That I may or may not have made up...)

1. A botanist studies plant life, yet someone who studies robots is not called a robotinist.
2. Since many cactuses have thorns, it probably hurts them to clap.
3. Four out of five people polled didn't know how to pluralize the word cactus and the fifth just kept yelling, "Get me down from here!".
4. Researchers suggest talking to your plants to help them grow, however the author says, gluing googly eyes on them will make them look more interested in what you're telling them.
5. There is an old legend (that I just made up) about why cactuses have spines. It's because after Queen Cactus's beloved husband passed away, she was so heartbroken that she decided she could never remarry. She covered herself in thorns so that no suiter could ever get close to her. To show their support for the queen, her loyal subjects, formed spines of their own. They soon regretted it because they could no longer show affection for one another. From then on, cacti expressed their love for one another, by growing flowers instead. The end. What are you waiting for the final credits? Move along to the next fact.
6. Cactuses grow in deserts, and one "s" made the difference between them lounging around in ice cream and cake or sweating all day in the heat. Boy, did they choose wrong!
7. Surprisingly, many cactus varieties grow flowers and yet are never seen in bouquets. I think it's because the roses would get jealous.
8. Cactus seeds come from porcupine quills.
9. You'd think since cactus live in the deserts, they would be thirsty and would like it, if you gave them more water but instead, they show their displeasure by dying.
10. I am not good at taking care of cactuses (see fact number 9).

This book is dedicated to everyone who has a tough time getting organized and an even tougher time remembering their password. I am grateful to the Lord for all he's done. A special thanks to Angel, who has a keen eye.

Herrera, Jessica R.
10 (Not So) Interesting Facts About Cactus(That I May or May Not Have Made Up)-A Password Book in Camouflage / written & illustrated by Jessica R. Herrera
-- U.S. 2019

ISBN 978-1-949915-12-9 (pbk.)
[1. Books—Personal Organizer. 2. Office Product. 3. Record Book.]
1. Herrera, Jessica R. I. Title.

JESSICA'S OTHER BOOKS INCLUDE:

The Bad Book

Bad Book Undercover: How Books Are Made

Bad Book vs. The Eraser: Color Your Adventure & Activity Book (K-1)

Bad Book vs. The Eraser: Color Your Adventure & Activity Book (2nd & Up)

Bad Book vs. The Eraser: Choose Your Adventure Comic Book

Bad Book's Day Off

Storyteller Book Developer Bible

What did you think about this book?
Leave a review and let the world know what you think. 😁

10 Not So Interesting Facts ABOUT CACTUS (That I may or may Not Have made up)

JessicaRHerrera.com

Passwords

Characactus: Captain Brambleton

A

Website: User Name:

Password 1:

Password 2:

Notes:

Security Question 1:

Answer 1:

Security Question 2:

Answer 2:

Security Question 3:

Answer 3:

Subscription? Y / N

Renewal Date:

Cost:

Website: User Name:

Password 1:

Password 2:

Notes:

Security Question 1:

Answer 1:

Security Question 2:

Answer 2:

Security Question 3:

Answer 3:

Subscription? Y / N

Renewal Date:

Cost:

Website: **User Name:**

Password 1:

Password 2:

Notes:

Security Question 1:

Answer 1:

Security Question 2:

Answer 2:

Security Question 3:

Answer 3:

Subscription? Y / N

Renewal Date:

Cost:

Website: **User Name:**

Password 1:

Password 2:

Notes:

Security Question 1:

Answer 1:

Security Question 2:

Answer 2:

Security Question 3:

Answer 3:

Subscription? Y / N

Renewal Date:

Cost:

10 Not So Interesting Facts About Cactus (That I may or may Not Have made Up)

A

Website: User Name:

Password 1:

Password 2:

Security Question 1:

Answer 1:

Security Question 2:

Answer 2:

Security Question 3:

Answer 3:

Notes:

Subscription? Y / N

Renewal Date:

Cost:

Website: User Name:

Password 1:

Password 2:

Security Question 1:

Answer 1:

Security Question 2:

Answer 2:

Security Question 3:

Answer 3:

Notes:

Subscription? Y / N

Renewal Date:

Cost:

Website: **User Name:**

Password 1:

Password 2:

Notes:

Security Question 1:

Answer 1:

Security Question 2:

Answer 2:

Security Question 3:

Answer 3:

Subscription? Y / N

Renewal Date:

Cost:

Website: **User Name:**

Password 1:

Password 2:

Notes:

Security Question 1:

Answer 1:

Security Question 2:

Answer 2:

Security Question 3:

Answer 3:

Subscription? Y / N

Renewal Date:

Cost:

10 Not So Interesting Facts About Cactus (That I may or may Not Have made Up)

A

Website: User Name:

Password 1:

Password 2:

Notes:

Security Question 1:

Answer 1:

Security Question 2:

Answer 2:

Security Question 3:

Answer 3:

Subscription? Y / N

Renewal Date:

Cost:

Website: User Name:

Password 1:

Password 2:

Notes:

Security Question 1:

Answer 1:

Security Question 2:

Answer 2:

Security Question 3:

Answer 3:

Subscription? Y / N

Renewal Date:

Cost:

A

Website: **User Name:**

Password 1:

Password 2:

Notes:

Security Question 1:

Answer 1:

Security Question 2:

Answer 2:

Security Question 3:

Answer 3:

Subscription? Y / N

Renewal Date:

Cost:

Website: **User Name:**

Password 1:

Password 2:

Notes:

Security Question 1:

Answer 1:

Security Question 2:

Answer 2:

Security Question 3:

Answer 3:

Subscription? Y / N

Renewal Date:

Cost:

A

Website: User Name:

Password 1:

Password 2:

Notes:

Security Question 1:

Answer 1:

Security Question 2:

Answer 2:

Security Question 3:

Answer 3:

Subscription? Y / N

Renewal Date:

Cost:

Website: User Name:

Password 1:

Password 2:

Notes:

Security Question 1:

Answer 1:

Security Question 2:

Answer 2:

Security Question 3:

Answer 3:

Subscription? Y / N

Renewal Date:

Cost:

B

Website: **User Name:**

Password 1:

Password 2:

Notes:

Security Question 1:

Answer 1:

Security Question 2:

Answer 2:

Security Question 3:

Answer 3:

Subscription? Y / N

Renewal Date:

Cost:

Website: **User Name:**

Password 1:

Password 2:

Notes:

Security Question 1:

Answer 1:

Security Question 2:

Answer 2:

Security Question 3:

Answer 3:

Subscription? Y / N

Renewal Date:

Cost:

B

Website: User Name:

Password 1:

Password 2:

Notes:

Security Question 1:

Answer 1:

Security Question 2:

Answer 2:

Security Question 3:

Answer 3:

Subscription? Y / N

Renewal Date:

Cost:

Website: User Name:

Password 1:

Password 2:

Notes:

Security Question 1:

Answer 1:

Security Question 2:

Answer 2:

Security Question 3:

Answer 3:

Subscription? Y / N

Renewal Date:

Cost:

B

Website: **User Name:**

Password 1: | | | | | | | | | | | | |

Password 2: | | | | | | | | | | | | |

Security Question 1:

Answer 1:

Security Question 2:

Answer 2:

Security Question 3:

Answer 3:

Notes: ______________________

Subscription? Y / N

Renewal Date: ______________________

Cost: ______________________

Website: **User Name:**

Password 1: | | | | | | | | | | | | |

Password 2: | | | | | | | | | | | | |

Security Question 1:

Answer 1:

Security Question 2:

Answer 2:

Security Question 3:

Answer 3:

Notes: ______________________

Subscription? Y / N

Renewal Date: ______________________

Cost: ______________________

B

Website: User Name:

Password 1:

Password 2:

Notes:

Security Question 1:

Answer 1:

Security Question 2:

Answer 2:

Security Question 3:

Answer 3:

Subscription? Y / N

Renewal Date:

Cost:

Website: User Name:

Password 1:

Password 2:

Notes:

Security Question 1:

Answer 1:

Security Question 2:

Answer 2:

Security Question 3:

Answer 3:

Subscription? Y / N

Renewal Date:

Cost:

B

Website: **User Name:**

Password 1: | | | | | | | | | | | | | |

Password 2: | | | | | | | | | | | | | |

Security Question 1:

Answer 1:

Security Question 2:

Answer 2:

Security Question 3:

Answer 3:

Notes:

Subscription? Y / N

Renewal Date:

Cost:

Website: **User Name:**

Password 1: | | | | | | | | | | | | | |

Password 2: | | | | | | | | | | | | | |

Security Question 1:

Answer 1:

Security Question 2:

Answer 2:

Security Question 3:

Answer 3:

Notes:

Subscription? Y / N

Renewal Date:

Cost:

B

Website: User Name:

Password 1:

Password 2:

Notes:

Security Question 1:

Answer 1:

Security Question 2:

Answer 2:

Security Question 3:

Answer 3:

Subscription? Y / N

Renewal Date:

Cost:

Website: User Name:

Password 1:

Password 2:

Notes:

Security Question 1:

Answer 1:

Security Question 2:

Answer 2:

Security Question 3:

Answer 3:

Subscription? Y / N

Renewal Date:

Cost:

Website: User Name:

Password 1:

Password 2:

Security Question 1:

Answer 1:

Security Question 2:

Answer 2:

Security Question 3:

Answer 3:

Notes:

Subscription? Y / N

Renewal Date:

Cost:

Website: User Name:

Password 1:

Password 2:

Security Question 1:

Answer 1:

Security Question 2:

Answer 2:

Security Question 3:

Answer 3:

Notes:

Subscription? Y / N

Renewal Date:

Cost:

C

Website: User Name:

Password 1:

Password 2:

Security Question 1:

Answer 1:

Security Question 2:

Answer 2:

Security Question 3:

Answer 3:

Notes:

Subscription? Y / N

Renewal Date:

Cost:

Website: User Name:

Password 1:

Password 2:

Security Question 1:

Answer 1:

Security Question 2:

Answer 2:

Security Question 3:

Answer 3:

Notes:

Subscription? Y / N

Renewal Date:

Cost:

Website: User Name:

Password 1:

Password 2:

Notes:

Security Question 1:

Answer 1:

Security Question 2:

Answer 2:

Security Question 3:

Answer 3:

Subscription? Y / N

Renewal Date:

Cost:

Website: User Name:

Password 1:

Password 2:

Notes:

Security Question 1:

Answer 1:

Security Question 2:

Answer 2:

Security Question 3:

Answer 3:

Subscription? Y / N

Renewal Date:

Cost:

10 Not So Interesting Facts ABOUT CACTUS (That I may or may Not Have made Up)

C

Website: User Name:

Password 1:

Password 2:

Security Question 1:

Answer 1:

Security Question 2:

Answer 2:

Security Question 3:

Answer 3:

Notes:

Subscription? Y / N

Renewal Date:

Cost:

Website: User Name:

Password 1:

Password 2:

Security Question 1:

Answer 1:

Security Question 2:

Answer 2:

Security Question 3:

Answer 3:

Notes:

Subscription? Y / N

Renewal Date:

Cost:

C

Website: User Name:

Password 1:

Password 2:

Notes:

Security Question 1:

Answer 1:

Security Question 2:

Answer 2:

Security Question 3:

Answer 3:

Subscription? Y / N

Renewal Date:

Cost:

Website: User Name:

Password 1:

Password 2:

Notes:

Security Question 1:

Answer 1:

Security Question 2:

Answer 2:

Security Question 3:

Answer 3:

Subscription? Y / N

Renewal Date:

Cost:

10 Not So Interesting Facts ABOUT CACTUS (That I may or may Not Have made Up)

C

C

Website: User Name:

Password 1:

Password 2:

Notes:

Security Question 1:

Answer 1:

Security Question 2:

Answer 2:

Security Question 3:

Answer 3:

Subscription? Y / N

Renewal Date:

Cost:

Website: User Name:

Password 1:

Password 2:

Notes:

Security Question 1:

Answer 1:

Security Question 2:

Answer 2:

Security Question 3:

Answer 3:

Subscription? Y / N

Renewal Date:

Cost:

Website: User Name:

Password 1:

Password 2:

Notes:

Security Question 1:

Answer 1:

Security Question 2:

Answer 2:

Security Question 3:

Answer 3:

Subscription? Y / N

Renewal Date:

Cost:

Website: User Name:

Password 1:

Password 2:

Notes:

Security Question 1:

Answer 1:

Security Question 2:

Answer 2:

Security Question 3:

Answer 3:

Subscription? Y / N

Renewal Date:

Cost:

D

Website: User Name:

Password 1:

Password 2:

Notes:

Security Question 1:

Answer 1:

Security Question 2:

Answer 2:

Security Question 3:

Answer 3:

Subscription? Y / N

Renewal Date:

Cost:

Website: User Name:

Password 1:

Password 2:

Notes:

Security Question 1:

Answer 1:

Security Question 2:

Answer 2:

Security Question 3:

Answer 3:

Subscription? Y / N

Renewal Date:

Cost:

D

Website: User Name:

Password 1:

Password 2:

Security Question 1:

Answer 1:

Security Question 2:

Answer 2:

Security Question 3:

Answer 3:

Notes:

Subscription? Y / N

Renewal Date:

Cost:

Website: User Name:

Password 1:

Password 2:

Security Question 1:

Answer 1:

Security Question 2:

Answer 2:

Security Question 3:

Answer 3:

Notes:

Subscription? Y / N

Renewal Date:

Cost:

10 Not So Interesting Facts ABOUT CACTUS (That I may or may Not Have made up)

D

Website: User Name:

Password 1:

Password 2:

Notes:

Security Question 1:

Answer 1:

Security Question 2:

Answer 2:

Security Question 3:

Answer 3:

Subscription? Y / N

Renewal Date:

Cost:

Website: User Name:

Password 1:

Password 2:

Notes:

Security Question 1:

Answer 1:

Security Question 2:

Answer 2:

Security Question 3:

Answer 3:

Subscription? Y / N

Renewal Date:

Cost:

Website: User Name:

Password 1:

Password 2:

Notes:

Security Question 1:

Answer 1:

Security Question 2:

Answer 2:

Security Question 3:

Subscription? Y / N

Renewal Date:

Answer 3:

Cost:

Website: User Name:

Password 1:

Password 2:

Notes:

Security Question 1:

Answer 1:

Security Question 2:

Answer 2:

Security Question 3:

Subscription? Y / N

Renewal Date:

Answer 3:

Cost:

Website: **User Name:**

Password 1:

Password 2:

Notes:

Security Question 1:

Answer 1:

E

Security Question 2:

Answer 2:

Security Question 3:

Subscription? Y / N

Renewal Date:

Answer 3:

Cost:

Website: **User Name:**

Password 1:

Password 2:

Notes:

Security Question 1:

Answer 1:

Security Question 2:

Answer 2:

Security Question 3:

Subscription? Y / N

Renewal Date:

Answer 3:

Cost:

Website: **User Name:**

Password 1:

Password 2:

Notes:

Security Question 1:

Answer 1:

Security Question 2:

Answer 2:

Security Question 3:

Answer 3:

Subscription? Y / N

Renewal Date:

Cost:

Website: **User Name:**

Password 1:

Password 2:

Notes:

Security Question 1:

Answer 1:

Security Question 2:

Answer 2:

Security Question 3:

Answer 3:

Subscription? Y / N

Renewal Date:

Cost:

E

E

Website: User Name:

Password 1:

Password 2:

Notes:

Security Question 1:

Answer 1:

Security Question 2:

Answer 2:

Security Question 3:

Answer 3:

Subscription? Y / N

Renewal Date:

Cost:

Website: User Name:

Password 1:

Password 2:

Notes:

Security Question 1:

Answer 1:

Security Question 2:

Answer 2:

Security Question 3:

Answer 3:

Subscription? Y / N

Renewal Date:

Cost:

Website: User Name:

Password 1: | | | | | | | | | | | | | |

Password 2: | | | | | | | | | | | | | |

Notes:

Security Question 1:

Answer 1:

Security Question 2:

Answer 2:

Security Question 3:

Subscription? Y / N

Renewal Date:

Answer 3:

Cost:

Website: User Name:

Password 1: | | | | | | | | | | | | | |

Password 2: | | | | | | | | | | | | | |

Notes:

Security Question 1:

Answer 1:

Security Question 2:

Answer 2:

Security Question 3:

Subscription? Y / N

Renewal Date:

Answer 3:

Cost:

E

Website: **User Name:**

Password 1:

Password 2:

Security Question 1:

Answer 1:

Security Question 2:

Answer 2:

Security Question 3:

Answer 3:

Notes:

Subscription? Y / N

Renewal Date:

Cost:

Website: **User Name:**

Password 1:

Password 2:

Security Question 1:

Answer 1:

Security Question 2:

Answer 2:

Security Question 3:

Answer 3:

Notes:

Subscription? Y / N

Renewal Date:

Cost:

Website: User Name:

Password 1:

Password 2:

Security Question 1:

Answer 1:

Security Question 2:

Answer 2:

Security Question 3:

Answer 3:

Notes:

Subscription? Y / N

Renewal Date:

Cost:

Website: User Name:

Password 1:

Password 2:

Security Question 1:

Answer 1:

Security Question 2:

Answer 2:

Security Question 3:

Answer 3:

Notes:

Subscription? Y / N

Renewal Date:

Cost:

F

F

Website: User Name:

Password 1:

Password 2:

Notes:

Security Question 1:

Answer 1:

Security Question 2:

Answer 2:

Security Question 3:

Answer 3:

Subscription? Y / N

Renewal Date:

Cost:

Website: User Name:

Password 1:

Password 2:

Notes:

Security Question 1:

Answer 1:

Security Question 2:

Answer 2:

Security Question 3:

Answer 3:

Subscription? Y / N

Renewal Date:

Cost:

Website: **User Name:**

Password 1: | | | | | | | | | | | | | |

Password 2: | | | | | | | | | | | | | |

Security Question 1:

Answer 1:

Security Question 2:

Answer 2:

Security Question 3:

Answer 3:

Notes:

Subscription? Y / N

Renewal Date:

Cost:

Website: **User Name:**

Password 1: | | | | | | | | | | | | | |

Password 2: | | | | | | | | | | | | | |

Security Question 1:

Answer 1:

Security Question 2:

Answer 2:

Security Question 3:

Answer 3:

Notes:

Subscription? Y / N

Renewal Date:

Cost:

F

F

Website: **User Name:**

Password 1:

Password 2:

Security Question 1:

Answer 1:

Security Question 2:

Answer 2:

Security Question 3:

Answer 3:

Notes:

Subscription? Y / N

Renewal Date:

Cost:

Website: **User Name:**

Password 1:

Password 2:

Security Question 1:

Answer 1:

Security Question 2:

Answer 2:

Security Question 3:

Answer 3:

Notes:

Subscription? Y / N

Renewal Date:

Cost:

Website: User Name:

Password 1:

Password 2:

Notes:

Security Question 1:

Answer 1:

Security Question 2:

Answer 2:

Security Question 3:

Answer 3:

Subscription? Y / N

Renewal Date:

Cost:

Website: User Name:

Password 1:

Password 2:

Notes:

Security Question 1:

Answer 1:

Security Question 2:

Answer 2:

Security Question 3:

Answer 3:

Subscription? Y / N

Renewal Date:

Cost:

F

F

Website: User Name:

Password 1:

Password 2:

Notes:

Security Question 1:

Answer 1:

Security Question 2:

Answer 2:

Security Question 3:

Answer 3:

Subscription? Y / N

Renewal Date:

Cost:

Website: User Name:

Password 1:

Password 2:

Notes:

Security Question 1:

Answer 1:

Security Question 2:

Answer 2:

Security Question 3:

Answer 3:

Subscription? Y / N

Renewal Date:

Cost:

Website: User Name:

Password 1:

Password 2:

Notes:

Security Question 1:

Answer 1:

Security Question 2:

Answer 2:

Security Question 3:

Subscription? Y / N

Renewal Date:

Answer 3:

Cost:

Website: User Name:

Password 1:

Password 2:

Notes:

Security Question 1:

Answer 1:

Security Question 2:

Answer 2:

Security Question 3:

Subscription? Y / N

Renewal Date:

Answer 3:

Cost:

10 Not So Interesting Facts ABOUT CACTUS (That I may or may Not Have made Up)

G

Website: User Name:

Password 1:

Password 2:

Security Question 1:

Answer 1:

Security Question 2:

Answer 2:

Security Question 3:

Answer 3:

Notes:

Subscription? Y / N

Renewal Date:

Cost:

G

Website: User Name:

Password 1:

Password 2:

Security Question 1:

Answer 1:

Security Question 2:

Answer 2:

Security Question 3:

Answer 3:

Notes:

Subscription? Y / N

Renewal Date:

Cost:

Website: User Name:

Password 1:

Password 2:

Notes:

Security Question 1:

Answer 1:

Security Question 2:

Answer 2:

Security Question 3:

Answer 3:

Subscription? Y / N

Renewal Date:

Cost:

Website: User Name:

Password 1:

Password 2:

Notes:

Security Question 1:

Answer 1:

Security Question 2:

Answer 2:

Security Question 3:

Answer 3:

Subscription? Y / N

Renewal Date:

Cost:

G

Website: User Name:

Password 1:

Password 2:

Notes:

Security Question 1:

Answer 1:

Security Question 2:

Answer 2:

Security Question 3:

Answer 3:

Subscription? Y / N

Renewal Date:

Cost:

Website: User Name:

Password 1:

Password 2:

Notes:

Security Question 1:

Answer 1:

Security Question 2:

Answer 2:

Security Question 3:

Answer 3:

Subscription? Y / N

Renewal Date:

Cost:

Website: **User Name:**

Password 1: | | | | | | | | | | | | |

Password 2: | | | | | | | | | | | | |

Security Question 1:

Answer 1:

Security Question 2:

Answer 2:

Security Question 3:

Answer 3:

Notes: ____________________

Subscription? Y / N

Renewal Date: ____________________

Cost: ____________________

Website: **User Name:**

Password 1: | | | | | | | | | | | | |

Password 2: | | | | | | | | | | | | |

Security Question 1:

Answer 1:

Security Question 2:

Answer 2:

Security Question 3:

Answer 3:

Notes: ____________________

Subscription? Y / N

Renewal Date: ____________________

Cost: ____________________

10 Not So Interesting Facts ABOUT CACTUS (That I may or may Not Have made Up)

G

G

Website: User Name:

Password 1:

Password 2:

Notes:

Security Question 1:

Answer 1:

Security Question 2:

Answer 2:

Security Question 3:

Answer 3:

Subscription? Y / N

Renewal Date:

Cost:

Website: User Name:

Password 1:

Password 2:

Notes:

Security Question 1:

Answer 1:

Security Question 2:

Answer 2:

Security Question 3:

Answer 3:

Subscription? Y / N

Renewal Date:

Cost:

Website: User Name:

Password 1:

Password 2:

Notes:

Security Question 1:

Answer 1:

Security Question 2:

Answer 2:

Security Question 3:

Answer 3:

Subscription? Y / N

Renewal Date:

Cost:

Website: User Name:

Password 1:

Password 2:

Notes:

Security Question 1:

Answer 1:

Security Question 2:

Answer 2:

Security Question 3:

Answer 3:

Subscription? Y / N

Renewal Date:

Cost:

H

10 Not So Interesting Facts ABOUT CACTUS (That I may or may Not Have made Up)

Website: User Name:

Password 1:

Password 2:

Notes:

Security Question 1:

Answer 1:

Security Question 2:

Answer 2:

Security Question 3:

Answer 3:

Subscription? Y / N

Renewal Date:

Cost:

Website: User Name:

Password 1:

Password 2:

Notes:

Security Question 1:

Answer 1:

Security Question 2:

Answer 2:

Security Question 3:

Answer 3:

Subscription? Y / N

Renewal Date:

Cost:

H

Website: User Name:

Password 1:

Password 2:

Notes:

Security Question 1:

Answer 1:

Security Question 2:

Answer 2:

Security Question 3:

Answer 3:

Subscription? Y / N

Renewal Date:

Cost:

Website: User Name:

Password 1:

Password 2:

Notes:

Security Question 1:

Answer 1:

Security Question 2:

Answer 2:

Security Question 3:

Answer 3:

Subscription? Y / N

Renewal Date:

Cost:

H

H

Website: User Name:

Password 1:

Password 2:

Security Question 1:

Answer 1:

Security Question 2:

Answer 2:

Security Question 3:

Answer 3:

Notes:

Subscription? Y / N

Renewal Date:

Cost:

Website: User Name:

Password 1:

Password 2:

Security Question 1:

Answer 1:

Security Question 2:

Answer 2:

Security Question 3:

Answer 3:

Notes:

Subscription? Y / N

Renewal Date:

Cost:

Website: **User Name:**

Password 1:

Password 2:

Notes:

Security Question 1:

Answer 1:

Security Question 2:

Answer 2:

Security Question 3:

Answer 3:

Subscription? Y / N

Renewal Date:

Cost:

I

Website: **User Name:**

Password 1:

Password 2:

Notes:

Security Question 1:

Answer 1:

Security Question 2:

Answer 2:

Security Question 3:

Answer 3:

Subscription? Y / N

Renewal Date:

Cost:

Website: User Name:

Password 1:

Password 2:

Notes:

Security Question 1:

Answer 1:

Security Question 2:

Answer 2:

Security Question 3:

Answer 3:

Subscription? Y / N

Renewal Date:

Cost:

Website: User Name:

Password 1:

Password 2:

Notes:

Security Question 1:

Answer 1:

Security Question 2:

Answer 2:

Security Question 3:

Answer 3:

Subscription? Y / N

Renewal Date:

Cost:

Website: **User Name:**

Password 1: | | | | | | | | | | | | | |

Password 2: | | | | | | | | | | | | | |

Notes:

Security Question 1:

Answer 1:

Security Question 2:

Answer 2:

Security Question 3:

Subscription? Y / N

Renewal Date:

Answer 3:

Cost:

Website: **User Name:**

Password 1: | | | | | | | | | | | | | |

Password 2: | | | | | | | | | | | | | |

Notes:

Security Question 1:

Answer 1:

Security Question 2:

Answer 2:

Security Question 3:

Subscription? Y / N

Renewal Date:

Answer 3:

Cost:

Website: **User Name:**

Password 1:

Password 2:

Security Question 1:

Answer 1:

Security Question 2:

Answer 2:

Security Question 3:

Answer 3:

Notes:

Subscription? Y / N

Renewal Date:

Cost:

Website: **User Name:**

Password 1:

Password 2:

Security Question 1:

Answer 1:

Security Question 2:

Answer 2:

Security Question 3:

Answer 3:

Notes:

Subscription? Y / N

Renewal Date:

Cost:

I

Website: **User Name:**

Password 1: | | | | | | | | | | | | | |

Password 2: | | | | | | | | | | | | | |

Security Question 1:

Answer 1:

Security Question 2:

Answer 2:

Security Question 3:

Answer 3:

Notes:

Subscription? Y / N

Renewal Date:

Cost:

J

Website: **User Name:**

Password 1: | | | | | | | | | | | | | |

Password 2: | | | | | | | | | | | | | |

Security Question 1:

Answer 1:

Security Question 2:

Answer 2:

Security Question 3:

Answer 3:

Notes:

Subscription? Y / N

Renewal Date:

Cost:

Website: User Name:

Password 1:

Password 2:

Security Question 1:

Answer 1:

Security Question 2:

Answer 2:

Security Question 3:

Answer 3:

Notes:

Subscription? Y / N

Renewal Date:

Cost:

J

Website: User Name:

Password 1:

Password 2:

Security Question 1:

Answer 1:

Security Question 2:

Answer 2:

Security Question 3:

Answer 3:

Notes:

Subscription? Y / N

Renewal Date:

Cost:

Website: User Name:

Password 1:

Password 2:

Notes:

Security Question 1:

Answer 1:

Security Question 2:

Answer 2:

Security Question 3:

Answer 3:

Subscription? Y / N

Renewal Date:

Cost:

J

Website: User Name:

Password 1:

Password 2:

Notes:

Security Question 1:

Answer 1:

Security Question 2:

Answer 2:

Security Question 3:

Answer 3:

Subscription? Y / N

Renewal Date:

Cost:

10 Not So Interesting Facts ABOUT CACTUS (That I may or may Not Have made Up)

Website: User Name:

Password 1:

Password 2:

Notes:

Security Question 1:

Answer 1:

Security Question 2:

Answer 2:

Security Question 3:

Answer 3:

Subscription? Y / N

Renewal Date:

Cost:

J

Website: User Name:

Password 1:

Password 2:

Notes:

Security Question 1:

Answer 1:

Security Question 2:

Answer 2:

Security Question 3:

Answer 3:

Subscription? Y / N

Renewal Date:

Cost:

Website: User Name:

Password 1: | | | | | | | | | | | | |

Password 2: | | | | | | | | | | | | |

Security Question 1:

Answer 1:

Security Question 2:

Answer 2:

Security Question 3:

Answer 3:

Notes:

Subscription? Y / N

Renewal Date:

Cost:

Website: User Name:

Password 1: | | | | | | | | | | | | |

Password 2: | | | | | | | | | | | | |

Security Question 1:

Answer 1:

Security Question 2:

Answer 2:

Security Question 3:

Answer 3:

Notes:

Subscription? Y / N

Renewal Date:

Cost:

K

Website: User Name:

Password 1:

Password 2:

Notes:

Security Question 1:

Answer 1:

Security Question 2:

Answer 2:

Security Question 3:

Answer 3:

Subscription? Y / N

Renewal Date:

Cost:

Website: User Name:

K

Password 1:

Password 2:

Notes:

Security Question 1:

Answer 1:

Security Question 2:

Answer 2:

Security Question 3:

Answer 3:

Subscription? Y / N

Renewal Date:

Cost:

Website: User Name:

Password 1:

Password 2:

Notes:

Security Question 1:

Answer 1:

Security Question 2:

Answer 2:

Security Question 3:

Answer 3:

Subscription? Y / N

Renewal Date:

Cost:

Website: User Name:

Password 1:

Password 2:

Notes:

Security Question 1:

Answer 1:

Security Question 2:

Answer 2:

Security Question 3:

Answer 3:

Subscription? Y / N

Renewal Date:

Cost:

Website: User Name:

Password 1:

Password 2:

Notes:

Security Question 1:

Answer 1:

Security Question 2:

Answer 2:

Security Question 3:

Answer 3:

Subscription? Y / N

Renewal Date:

Cost:

Website: User Name:

K

Password 1:

Password 2:

Notes:

Security Question 1:

Answer 1:

Security Question 2:

Answer 2:

Security Question 3:

Answer 3:

Subscription? Y / N

Renewal Date:

Cost:

Website: User Name:

Password 1:

Password 2:

Notes:

Security Question 1:

Answer 1:

Security Question 2:

Answer 2:

Security Question 3:

Subscription? Y / N

Renewal Date:

Answer 3:

Cost:

Website: User Name:

Password 1:

Password 2:

Notes:

Security Question 1:

Answer 1:

Security Question 2:

Answer 2:

Security Question 3:

Subscription? Y / N

Renewal Date:

Answer 3:

Cost:

Website: User Name:

Password 1:

Password 2:

Notes:

Security Question 1:

Answer 1:

Security Question 2:

Answer 2:

Security Question 3:

Answer 3:

Subscription? Y / N

Renewal Date:

Cost:

Website: User Name:

Password 1:

Password 2:

Notes:

Security Question 1:

Answer 1:

Security Question 2:

Answer 2:

Security Question 3:

Answer 3:

Subscription? Y / N

Renewal Date:

Cost:

L

Website: User Name:

Password 1:

Password 2:

Notes:

Security Question 1:

Answer 1:

Security Question 2:

Answer 2:

Security Question 3:

Answer 3:

Subscription? Y / N

Renewal Date:

Cost:

Website: User Name:

Password 1:

Password 2:

Notes:

Security Question 1:

Answer 1:

Security Question 2:

Answer 2:

Security Question 3:

Answer 3:

Subscription? Y / N

Renewal Date:

Cost:

L

Website: User Name:

Password 1:

Password 2:

Notes:

Security Question 1:

Answer 1:

Security Question 2:

Answer 2:

Security Question 3:

Answer 3:

Subscription? Y / N

Renewal Date:

Cost:

Website: User Name:

Password 1:

Password 2:

Notes:

Security Question 1:

Answer 1:

Security Question 2:

Answer 2:

Security Question 3:

Answer 3:

Subscription? Y / N

Renewal Date:

Cost:

L

Website: User Name:

Password 1:

Password 2:

Notes:

Security Question 1:

Answer 1:

Security Question 2:

Answer 2:

Security Question 3:

Answer 3:

Subscription? Y / N

Renewal Date:

Cost:

Website: User Name:

Password 1:

Password 2:

Notes:

Security Question 1:

Answer 1:

Security Question 2:

Answer 2:

Security Question 3:

Answer 3:

Subscription? Y / N

Renewal Date:

Cost:

M

Website: User Name:

Password 1:

Password 2:

Notes:

Security Question 1:

Answer 1:

Security Question 2:

Answer 2:

Security Question 3:

Answer 3:

Subscription? Y / N

Renewal Date:

Cost:

Website: User Name:

Password 1:

Password 2:

Notes:

Security Question 1:

Answer 1:

Security Question 2:

Answer 2:

Security Question 3:

Answer 3:

Subscription? Y / N

Renewal Date:

Cost:

M

Website: **User Name:**

Password 1: | | | | | | | | | | | | |

Password 2: | | | | | | | | | | | | |

Security Question 1:

Answer 1:

Security Question 2:

Answer 2:

Security Question 3:

Answer 3:

Notes:

Subscription? Y / N

Renewal Date:

Cost:

Website: **User Name:**

Password 1: | | | | | | | | | | | | |

Password 2: | | | | | | | | | | | | |

Security Question 1:

Answer 1:

Security Question 2:

Answer 2:

Security Question 3:

Answer 3:

Notes:

Subscription? Y / N

Renewal Date:

Cost:

M

Website: User Name:

Password 1:

Password 2:

Notes:

Security Question 1:

Answer 1:

Security Question 2:

Answer 2:

Security Question 3:

Answer 3:

Subscription? Y / N

Renewal Date:

Cost:

Website: User Name:

Password 1:

Password 2:

Notes:

Security Question 1:

Answer 1:

Security Question 2:

Answer 2:

Security Question 3:

Answer 3:

Subscription? Y / N

Renewal Date:

Cost:

M

Website: User Name:

Password 1:

Password 2:

Security Question 1:

Answer 1:

Security Question 2:

Answer 2:

Security Question 3:

Answer 3:

Notes:

Subscription? Y / N

Renewal Date:

Cost:

Website: User Name:

Password 1:

Password 2:

Security Question 1:

Answer 1:

Security Question 2:

Answer 2:

Security Question 3:

Answer 3:

Notes:

Subscription? Y / N

Renewal Date:

Cost:

Website: User Name:

Password 1:

Password 2:

Security Question 1:

Answer 1:

Security Question 2:

Answer 2:

Security Question 3:

Answer 3:

Notes:

Subscription? Y / N

Renewal Date:

Cost:

Website: User Name:

Password 1:

Password 2:

Security Question 1:

Answer 1:

Security Question 2:

Answer 2:

Security Question 3:

Answer 3:

Notes:

Subscription? Y / N

Renewal Date:

Cost:

N

Website: User Name:

Password 1:

Password 2:

Notes:

Security Question 1:

Answer 1:

Security Question 2:

Answer 2:

Security Question 3:

Answer 3:

Subscription? Y / N

Renewal Date:

Cost:

Website: User Name:

Password 1:

Password 2:

Notes:

Security Question 1:

Answer 1:

Security Question 2:

Answer 2:

Security Question 3:

Answer 3:

Subscription? Y / N

Renewal Date:

Cost:

N

Website: User Name:

Password 1:

Password 2:

Notes:

Security Question 1:

Answer 1:

Security Question 2:

Answer 2:

Security Question 3:

Answer 3:

Subscription? Y / N

Renewal Date:

Cost:

Website: User Name:

Password 1:

Password 2:

Notes:

Security Question 1:

Answer 1:

Security Question 2:

Answer 2:

Security Question 3:

Answer 3:

Subscription? Y / N

Renewal Date:

Cost:

N

Website: User Name:

Password 1:

Password 2:

Notes:

Security Question 1:

Answer 1:

Security Question 2:

Answer 2:

Security Question 3:

Answer 3:

Subscription? Y / N

Renewal Date:

Cost:

Website: User Name:

Password 1:

Password 2:

Notes:

Security Question 1:

Answer 1:

Security Question 2:

Answer 2:

Security Question 3:

Answer 3:

Subscription? Y / N

Renewal Date:

Cost:

Website: User Name:

Password 1:

Password 2:

Notes:

Security Question 1:

Answer 1:

Security Question 2:

Answer 2:

Security Question 3:

Subscription? Y / N

Renewal Date:

Answer 3:

Cost:

Website: User Name:

Password 1:

Password 2:

Notes:

Security Question 1:

Answer 1:

O

Security Question 2:

Answer 2:

Security Question 3:

Subscription? Y / N

Renewal Date:

Answer 3:

Cost:

Website: **User Name:**

Password 1:													
Password 2:													

Security Question 1:

Answer 1:

Security Question 2:

Answer 2:

Security Question 3:

Answer 3:

Notes:

Subscription? Y / N

Renewal Date:

Cost:

Website: **User Name:**

Password 1:													
Password 2:													

Security Question 1:

Answer 1:

Security Question 2:

Answer 2:

Security Question 3:

Answer 3:

Notes:

Subscription? Y / N

Renewal Date:

Cost:

Website: User Name:

Password 1:

Password 2:

Notes:

Security Question 1:

Answer 1:

Security Question 2:

Answer 2:

Security Question 3:

Answer 3:

Subscription? Y / N

Renewal Date:

Cost:

Website: User Name:

Password 1:

Password 2:

Notes:

Security Question 1:

Answer 1:

Security Question 2:

Answer 2:

Security Question 3:

Answer 3:

Subscription? Y / N

Renewal Date:

Cost:

O

Website: **User Name:**

Password 1:

Password 2:

Security Question 1:

Answer 1:

Security Question 2:

Answer 2:

Security Question 3:

Answer 3:

Notes:

Subscription? Y / N

Renewal Date:

Cost:

Website: **User Name:**

Password 1:

Password 2:

Security Question 1:

Answer 1:

Security Question 2:

Answer 2:

Security Question 3:

Answer 3:

Notes:

Subscription? Y / N

Renewal Date:

Cost:

P

Website: User Name:

Password 1:

Password 2:

Notes:

Security Question 1:

Answer 1:

Security Question 2:

Answer 2:

Security Question 3:

Subscription? Y / N

Renewal Date:

Answer 3:

Cost:

Website: User Name:

Password 1:

Password 2:

Notes:

Security Question 1:

Answer 1:

Security Question 2:

P

Answer 2:

Security Question 3:

Subscription? Y / N

Renewal Date:

Answer 3:

Cost:

Website: **User Name:**

Password 1: | | | | | | | | | | | | |

Password 2: | | | | | | | | | | | | |

Security Question 1:

Answer 1:

Security Question 2:

Answer 2:

Security Question 3:

Answer 3:

Notes:

Subscription? Y / N

Renewal Date:

Cost:

Website: **User Name:**

Password 1: | | | | | | | | | | | | |

Password 2: | | | | | | | | | | | | |

Security Question 1:

Answer 1:

Security Question 2:

Answer 2:

Security Question 3:

Answer 3:

Notes:

Subscription? Y / N

Renewal Date:

Cost:

P

Website: User Name:

Password 1:

Password 2:

Security Question 1:

Answer 1:

Security Question 2:

Answer 2:

Security Question 3:

Answer 3:

Notes:

Subscription? Y / N

Renewal Date:

Cost:

Website: User Name:

Password 1:

Password 2:

Security Question 1:

Answer 1:

Security Question 2:

Answer 2:

Security Question 3:

Answer 3:

Notes:

Subscription? Y / N

Renewal Date:

Cost:

P

Website: **User Name:**

Password 1:

Password 2:

Notes:

Security Question 1:

Answer 1:

Security Question 2:

Answer 2:

Security Question 3:

Answer 3:

Subscription? Y / N

Renewal Date:

Cost:

Website: **User Name:**

Password 1:

Password 2:

Notes:

Security Question 1:

Answer 1:

Security Question 2:

Answer 2:

Security Question 3:

Answer 3:

Subscription? Y / N

Renewal Date:

Cost:

P

Website: User Name:

Password 1:

Password 2:

Notes:

Security Question 1:

Answer 1:

Security Question 2:

Answer 2:

Security Question 3:

Answer 3:

Subscription? Y / N

Renewal Date:

Cost:

Website: User Name:

Password 1:

Password 2:

Notes:

Security Question 1:

Answer 1:

Security Question 2:

Answer 2:

Security Question 3:

Answer 3:

Subscription? Y / N

Renewal Date:

Cost:

Q

Website: User Name:

Password 1:

Password 2:

Notes:

Security Question 1:

Answer 1:

Security Question 2:

Answer 2:

Security Question 3:

Answer 3:

Subscription? Y / N

Renewal Date:

Cost:

Website: User Name:

Password 1:

Password 2:

Notes:

Security Question 1:

Answer 1:

Security Question 2:

Answer 2:

Security Question 3:

Answer 3:

Subscription? Y / N

Renewal Date:

Cost:

Q

Website: User Name:

Password 1:

Password 2:

Notes:

Security Question 1:

Answer 1:

Security Question 2:

Answer 2:

Security Question 3:

Subscription? Y / N

Renewal Date:

Answer 3:

Cost:

Website: User Name:

Password 1:

Password 2:

Notes:

Security Question 1:

Answer 1:

Security Question 2:

Answer 2:

Q

Security Question 3:

Subscription? Y / N

Renewal Date:

Answer 3:

Cost:

Website: User Name:

Password 1:

Password 2:

Notes:

Security Question 1:

Answer 1:

Security Question 2:

Answer 2:

Security Question 3:

Answer 3:

Subscription? Y / N

Renewal Date:

Cost:

Website: User Name:

Password 1:

Password 2:

Notes:

Security Question 1:

Answer 1:

Security Question 2:

Answer 2:

Security Question 3:

Answer 3:

Subscription? Y / N

Renewal Date:

Cost:

R

10 Not So Interesting Facts ABOUT CACTUS (That I may or may Not Have made Up)

Website: User Name:

Password 1:

Password 2:

Notes:

Security Question 1:

Answer 1:

Security Question 2:

Answer 2:

Security Question 3:

Answer 3:

Subscription? Y / N

Renewal Date:

Cost:

Website: User Name:

Password 1:

Password 2:

Notes:

Security Question 1:

Answer 1:

Security Question 2:

Answer 2:

Security Question 3:

Answer 3:

Subscription? Y / N

Renewal Date:

Cost:

R

Website: **User Name:**

Password 1: | | | | | | | | | | | | | |

Password 2: | | | | | | | | | | | | | |

Security Question 1:

Answer 1:

Security Question 2:

Answer 2:

Security Question 3:

Answer 3:

Notes: ____________________

Subscription? Y / N

Renewal Date: ____________________

Cost: ____________________

Website: **User Name:**

Password 1: | | | | | | | | | | | | | |

Password 2: | | | | | | | | | | | | | |

Security Question 1:

Answer 1:

Security Question 2:

Answer 2:

Security Question 3:

Answer 3:

Notes: ____________________

Subscription? Y / N

Renewal Date: ____________________

Cost: ____________________

R

Website: User Name:

Password 1:

Password 2:

Notes:

Security Question 1:

Answer 1:

Security Question 2:

Answer 2:

Security Question 3:

Answer 3:

Subscription? Y / N

Renewal Date:

Cost:

Website: User Name:

Password 1:

Password 2:

Notes:

Security Question 1:

Answer 1:

Security Question 2:

Answer 2:

Security Question 3:

Answer 3:

Subscription? Y / N

Renewal Date:

Cost:

R

Website: User Name:

Password 1:

Password 2:

Security Question 1:

Answer 1:

Security Question 2:

Answer 2:

Security Question 3:

Answer 3:

Notes:

Subscription? Y / N

Renewal Date:

Cost:

Website: User Name:

Password 1:

Password 2:

Security Question 1:

Answer 1:

Security Question 2:

Answer 2:

Security Question 3:

Answer 3:

Notes:

Subscription? Y / N

Renewal Date:

Cost:

R

10 Not So Interesting Facts ABOUT CACTUS (That I may or may Not Have made up)

Website: **User Name:**

Password 1: | | | | | | | | | | | | | |

Password 2: | | | | | | | | | | | | | |

Security Question 1:

Answer 1:

Security Question 2:

Answer 2:

Security Question 3:

Answer 3:

Notes: ____

Subscription? Y / N

Renewal Date: ____

Cost: ____

Website: **User Name:**

Password 1: | | | | | | | | | | | | | |

Password 2: | | | | | | | | | | | | | |

Security Question 1:

Answer 1:

Security Question 2:

Answer 2:

Security Question 3:

Answer 3:

Notes: ____

Subscription? Y / N

Renewal Date: ____

Cost: ____

R

Website: User Name:

Password 1:

Password 2:

Notes:

Security Question 1:

Answer 1:

Security Question 2:

Answer 2:

Security Question 3:

Answer 3:

Subscription? Y / N

Renewal Date:

Cost:

Website: User Name:

Password 1:

Password 2:

Notes:

Security Question 1:

Answer 1:

Security Question 2:

Answer 2:

Security Question 3:

Answer 3:

Subscription? Y / N

Renewal Date:

Cost:

Website: User Name:

Password 1:

Password 2:

Notes:

Security Question 1:

Answer 1:

Security Question 2:

Answer 2:

Security Question 3:

Answer 3:

Subscription? Y / N

Renewal Date:

Cost:

Website: User Name:

Password 1:

Password 2:

Notes:

Security Question 1:

Answer 1:

Security Question 2:

Answer 2:

Security Question 3:

Answer 3:

Subscription? Y / N

Renewal Date:

Cost:

S

Website: User Name:

Password 1: | | | | | | | | | | | | | |

Password 2: | | | | | | | | | | | | | |

Notes:

Security Question 1:

Answer 1:

Security Question 2:

Answer 2:

Security Question 3:

Answer 3:

Subscription? Y / N

Renewal Date:

Cost:

Website: User Name:

Password 1: | | | | | | | | | | | | | |

Password 2: | | | | | | | | | | | | | |

Notes:

Security Question 1:

Answer 1:

Security Question 2:

Answer 2:

Security Question 3:

Answer 3:

Subscription? Y / N

Renewal Date:

Cost:

Website: User Name:

Password 1:

Password 2:

Notes:

Security Question 1:

Answer 1:

Security Question 2:

Answer 2:

Security Question 3:

Answer 3:

Subscription? Y / N

Renewal Date:

Cost:

Website: User Name:

Password 1:

Password 2:

Notes:

Security Question 1:

Answer 1:

Security Question 2:

Answer 2:

Security Question 3:

Answer 3:

Subscription? Y / N

Renewal Date:

Cost:

Website: **User Name:**

Password 1:

Password 2:

Notes:

Security Question 1:

Answer 1:

Security Question 2:

Answer 2:

Security Question 3:

Subscription? Y / N

Renewal Date:

Answer 3:

Cost:

Website: **User Name:**

Password 1:

Password 2:

Notes:

Security Question 1:

Answer 1:

Security Question 2:

Answer 2:

Security Question 3:

Subscription? Y / N

Renewal Date:

Answer 3:

Cost:

10 Not so Interesting Facts About Cactus (That I may or may Not Have made Up)

S

T

Website: User Name:

Password 1:

Password 2:

Security Question 1:

Answer 1:

Security Question 2:

Answer 2:

Security Question 3:

Answer 3:

Notes:

Subscription? Y / N

Renewal Date:

Cost:

Website: User Name:

Password 1:

Password 2:

Security Question 1:

Answer 1:

Security Question 2:

Answer 2:

Security Question 3:

Answer 3:

Notes:

Subscription? Y / N

Renewal Date:

Cost:

Website: User Name:

Password 1:

Password 2:

Notes:

Security Question 1:

Answer 1:

Security Question 2:

Answer 2:

Security Question 3:

Subscription? Y / N

Renewal Date:

Answer 3:

Cost:

Website: User Name:

Password 1:

Password 2:

Notes:

Security Question 1:

Answer 1:

Security Question 2:

Answer 2:

Security Question 3:

Subscription? Y / N

Renewal Date:

Answer 3:

Cost:

10 Not So Interesting Facts ABOUT CACTUS (That I may or may Not Have made Up)

T

Website: User Name:

Password 1:

Password 2:

Notes:

Security Question 1:

Answer 1:

Security Question 2:

Answer 2:

Security Question 3:

Answer 3:

Subscription? Y / N

Renewal Date:

Cost:

Website: User Name:

Password 1:

Password 2:

Notes:

Security Question 1:

Answer 1:

Security Question 2:

Answer 2:

Security Question 3:

Answer 3:

Subscription? Y / N

Renewal Date:

Cost:

Website: User Name:

Password 1:

Password 2:

Notes:

Security Question 1:

Answer 1:

Security Question 2:

Answer 2:

Security Question 3:

Answer 3:

Subscription? Y / N

Renewal Date:

Cost:

Website: User Name:

Password 1:

Password 2:

Notes:

Security Question 1:

Answer 1:

Security Question 2:

Answer 2:

Security Question 3:

Answer 3:

Subscription? Y / N

Renewal Date:

Cost:

T

Website: User Name:

Password 1:

Password 2:

Security Question 1:

Answer 1:

Security Question 2:

Answer 2:

Security Question 3:

Answer 3:

Notes:

Subscription? Y / N

Renewal Date:

Cost:

Website: User Name:

Password 1:

Password 2:

Security Question 1:

Answer 1:

Security Question 2:

Answer 2:

Security Question 3:

Answer 3:

Notes:

Subscription? Y / N

Renewal Date:

Cost:

U

Website: User Name:

Password 1:

Password 2:

Notes:

Security Question 1:

Answer 1:

Security Question 2:

Answer 2:

Security Question 3:

Answer 3:

Subscription? Y / N

Renewal Date:

Cost:

Website: User Name:

Password 1:

Password 2:

Notes:

Security Question 1:

Answer 1:

Security Question 2:

Answer 2:

Security Question 3:

Answer 3:

Subscription? Y / N

Renewal Date:

Cost:

U

Website: User Name:

Password 1:

Password 2:

Notes:

Security Question 1:

Answer 1:

Security Question 2:

Answer 2:

Security Question 3:

Answer 3:

Subscription? Y / N

Renewal Date:

Cost:

Website: User Name:

Password 1:

Password 2:

Notes:

Security Question 1:

Answer 1:

Security Question 2:

Answer 2:

Security Question 3:

Answer 3:

Subscription? Y / N

Renewal Date:

Cost:

U

Website: User Name:

Password 1:

Password 2:

Notes:

Security Question 1:

Answer 1:

Security Question 2:

Answer 2:

Security Question 3:

Answer 3:

Subscription? Y / N

Renewal Date:

Cost:

Website: User Name:

Password 1:

Password 2:

Notes:

Security Question 1:

Answer 1:

Security Question 2:

Answer 2:

Security Question 3:

Answer 3:

Subscription? Y / N

Renewal Date:

Cost:

U

Website: User Name:

Password 1:

Password 2:

Notes:

Security Question 1:

Answer 1:

Security Question 2:

Answer 2:

Security Question 3:

Answer 3:

Subscription? Y / N

Renewal Date:

Cost:

Website: User Name:

Password 1:

Password 2:

Notes:

Security Question 1:

Answer 1:

Security Question 2:

Answer 2:

Security Question 3:

Answer 3:

Subscription? Y / N

Renewal Date:

Cost:

Website: **User Name:**

Password 1: | | | | | | | | | | | | | |

Password 2: | | | | | | | | | | | | | |

Security Question 1:

Answer 1:

Security Question 2:

Answer 2:

Security Question 3:

Answer 3:

Notes: ______

Subscription? Y / N

Renewal Date: ______

Cost: ______

Website: **User Name:**

Password 1: | | | | | | | | | | | | | |

Password 2: | | | | | | | | | | | | | |

Security Question 1:

Answer 1:

Security Question 2:

Answer 2:

Security Question 3:

Answer 3:

Notes: ______

Subscription? Y / N

Renewal Date: ______

Cost: ______

V

V

Website: User Name:

Password 1:

Password 2:

Notes:

Security Question 1:

Answer 1:

Security Question 2:

Answer 2:

Security Question 3:

Answer 3:

Subscription? Y / N

Renewal Date:

Cost:

Website: User Name:

Password 1:

Password 2:

Notes:

Security Question 1:

Answer 1:

Security Question 2:

Answer 2:

Security Question 3:

Answer 3:

Subscription? Y / N

Renewal Date:

Cost:

V

Website: User Name:

Password 1:

Password 2:

Notes:

Security Question 1:

Answer 1:

Security Question 2:

Answer 2:

Security Question 3:

Answer 3:

Subscription? Y / N

Renewal Date:

Cost:

Website: User Name:

Password 1:

Password 2:

Notes:

Security Question 1:

Answer 1:

Security Question 2:

Answer 2:

Security Question 3:

Answer 3:

Subscription? Y / N

Renewal Date:

Cost:

V

Website: User Name:

Password 1:

Password 2:

Notes:

Security Question 1:

Answer 1:

Security Question 2:

Answer 2:

Security Question 3:

Answer 3:

Subscription? Y / N

Renewal Date:

Cost:

Website: User Name:

Password 1:

Password 2:

Notes:

Security Question 1:

Answer 1:

Security Question 2:

Answer 2:

Security Question 3:

Answer 3:

Subscription? Y / N

Renewal Date:

Cost:

Website: User Name:

Password 1:

Password 2:

Notes:

Security Question 1:

Answer 1:

Security Question 2:

Answer 2:

Security Question 3:

Answer 3:

Subscription? Y / N

Renewal Date:

Cost:

Website: User Name:

Password 1:

Password 2:

Notes:

Security Question 1:

Answer 1:

Security Question 2:

Answer 2:

Security Question 3:

Answer 3:

Subscription? Y / N

Renewal Date:

Cost:

W

W

Website: User Name:

Password 1:

Password 2:

Notes:

Security Question 1:

Answer 1:

Security Question 2:

Answer 2:

Security Question 3:

Answer 3:

Subscription? Y / N

Renewal Date:

Cost:

Website: User Name:

Password 1:

Password 2:

Notes:

Security Question 1:

Answer 1:

Security Question 2:

Answer 2:

Security Question 3:

Answer 3:

Subscription? Y / N

Renewal Date:

Cost:

Website: User Name:

Password 1:

Password 2:

Notes:

Security Question 1:

Answer 1:

Security Question 2:

Answer 2:

Security Question 3:

Answer 3:

Subscription? Y / N

Renewal Date:

Cost:

Website: User Name:

Password 1:

Password 2:

Notes:

Security Question 1:

Answer 1:

Security Question 2:

Answer 2:

Security Question 3:

Answer 3:

Subscription? Y / N

Renewal Date:

Cost:

W

Website: User Name:

Password 1:

Password 2:

Security Question 1:

Answer 1:

Security Question 2:

Answer 2:

Security Question 3:

Answer 3:

Notes:

Subscription? Y / N

Renewal Date:

Cost:

Website: User Name:

Password 1:

Password 2:

Security Question 1:

Answer 1:

Security Question 2:

Answer 2:

Security Question 3:

Answer 3:

Notes:

Subscription? Y / N

Renewal Date:

Cost:

Website: User Name:

Password 1:

Password 2:

Security Question 1:

Answer 1:

Security Question 2:

Answer 2:

Security Question 3:

Answer 3:

Notes:

Subscription? Y / N

Renewal Date:

Cost:

Website: User Name:

Password 1:

Password 2:

Security Question 1:

Answer 1:

Security Question 2:

Answer 2:

Security Question 3:

Answer 3:

Notes:

Subscription? Y / N

Renewal Date:

Cost:

10 Not So Interesting Facts ABOUT CACTUS (That I may or may Not Have made up)

X

X

Website: User Name:

Password 1:

Password 2:

Notes:

Security Question 1:

Answer 1:

Security Question 2:

Answer 2:

Security Question 3:

Answer 3:

Subscription? Y / N

Renewal Date:

Cost:

Website: User Name:

Password 1:

Password 2:

Notes:

Security Question 1:

Answer 1:

Security Question 2:

Answer 2:

Security Question 3:

Answer 3:

Subscription? Y / N

Renewal Date:

Cost:

Website: User Name:

Password 1:

Password 2:

Notes:

Security Question 1:

Answer 1:

Security Question 2:

Answer 2:

Security Question 3:

Subscription? Y / N

Renewal Date:

Answer 3:

Cost:

Website: User Name:

Password 1:

Password 2:

Notes:

Security Question 1:

Answer 1:

Security Question 2:

Answer 2:

Security Question 3:

Subscription? Y / N

Renewal Date:

Answer 3:

Cost:

X

Website: User Name:

Password 1:

Password 2:

Notes:

Security Question 1:

Answer 1:

Security Question 2:

Answer 2:

Security Question 3:

Answer 3:

Subscription? Y / N

Renewal Date:

Cost:

Website: User Name:

Password 1:

Password 2:

Notes:

Security Question 1:

Answer 1:

Security Question 2:

Answer 2:

Security Question 3:

Answer 3:

Subscription? Y / N

Renewal Date:

Cost:

Website: User Name:

Password 1:

Password 2:

Notes:

Security Question 1:

Answer 1:

Security Question 2:

Answer 2:

Security Question 3:

Answer 3:

Subscription? Y / N

Renewal Date:

Cost:

Website: User Name:

Password 1:

Password 2:

Notes:

Security Question 1:

Answer 1:

Security Question 2:

Answer 2:

Security Question 3:

Answer 3:

Subscription? Y / N

Renewal Date:

Cost:

Y

Website: User Name:

Password 1:

Password 2:

Notes:

Security Question 1:

Answer 1:

Security Question 2:

Answer 2:

Security Question 3:

Answer 3:

Subscription? Y / N

Renewal Date:

Cost:

Website: User Name:

Password 1:

Password 2:

Notes:

Security Question 1:

Answer 1:

Security Question 2:

Answer 2:

Security Question 3:

Answer 3:

Subscription? Y / N

Renewal Date:

Cost:

Website: User Name:

Password 1:

Password 2:

Notes:

Security Question 1:

Answer 1:

Security Question 2:

Answer 2:

Security Question 3:

Answer 3:

Subscription? Y / N

Renewal Date:

Cost:

Website: User Name:

Password 1:

Password 2:

Notes:

Security Question 1:

Answer 1:

Security Question 2:

Answer 2:

Security Question 3:

Answer 3:

Subscription? Y / N

Renewal Date:

Cost:

10 Not So Interesting Facts About Cactus (That I may or may Not Have made up)

Y

Y

Website: User Name:

Password 1:

Password 2:

Security Question 1:

Answer 1:

Security Question 2:

Answer 2:

Security Question 3:

Answer 3:

Notes:

Subscription? Y / N

Renewal Date:

Cost:

Website: User Name:

Password 1:

Password 2:

Security Question 1:

Answer 1:

Security Question 2:

Answer 2:

Security Question 3:

Answer 3:

Notes:

Subscription? Y / N

Renewal Date:

Cost:

Website: User Name:

Password 1: | | | | | | | | | | | | |

Password 2: | | | | | | | | | | | | |

Security Question 1:

Answer 1:

Security Question 2:

Answer 2:

Security Question 3:

Answer 3:

Notes: ______

Subscription? Y / N

Renewal Date: ______

Cost: ______

Website: User Name:

Password 1: | | | | | | | | | | | | |

Password 2: | | | | | | | | | | | | |

Security Question 1:

Answer 1:

Security Question 2:

Answer 2:

Security Question 3:

Answer 3:

Notes: ______

Subscription? Y / N

Renewal Date: ______

Cost: ______

10 Not So Interesting Facts ABOUT CACTUS (That I may or may Not Have made up)

Z

Z

Website: User Name:

Password 1:

Password 2:

Notes:

Security Question 1:

Answer 1:

Security Question 2:

Answer 2:

Security Question 3:

Answer 3:

Subscription? Y / N

Renewal Date:

Cost:

Website: User Name:

Password 1:

Password 2:

Notes:

Security Question 1:

Answer 1:

Security Question 2:

Answer 2:

Security Question 3:

Answer 3:

Subscription? Y / N

Renewal Date:

Cost:

Website: User Name:

Password 1:

Password 2:

Security Question 1:

Answer 1:

Security Question 2:

Answer 2:

Security Question 3:

Answer 3:

Notes:

Subscription? Y / N

Renewal Date:

Cost:

Website: User Name:

Password 1:

Password 2:

Security Question 1:

Answer 1:

Security Question 2:

Answer 2:

Security Question 3:

Answer 3:

Notes:

Subscription? Y / N

Renewal Date:

Cost:

10 Not So Interesting Facts ABOUT CACTUS (That I may or may Not Have made up)

Z

Z

Website: User Name:

Password 1:

Password 2:

Notes:

Security Question 1:

Answer 1:

Security Question 2:

Answer 2:

Security Question 3:

Answer 3:

Subscription? Y / N

Renewal Date:

Cost:

Website: User Name:

Password 1:

Password 2:

Notes:

Security Question 1:

Answer 1:

Security Question 2:

Answer 2:

Security Question 3:

Answer 3:

Subscription? Y / N

Renewal Date:

Cost:

Notes

Characactus: Franken Creeper

Notes

Have you been put on hold forever? Were you sucked into a never-ending unstimulating conversation? Then doodle your own characactus design below and let the creativity flow.

NOTES

Notes

Notes

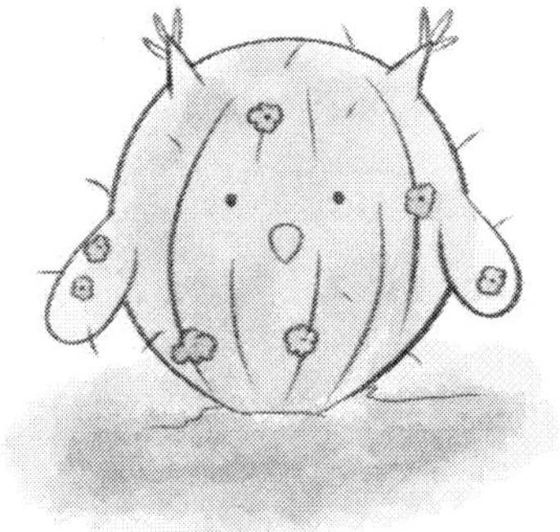

Notes

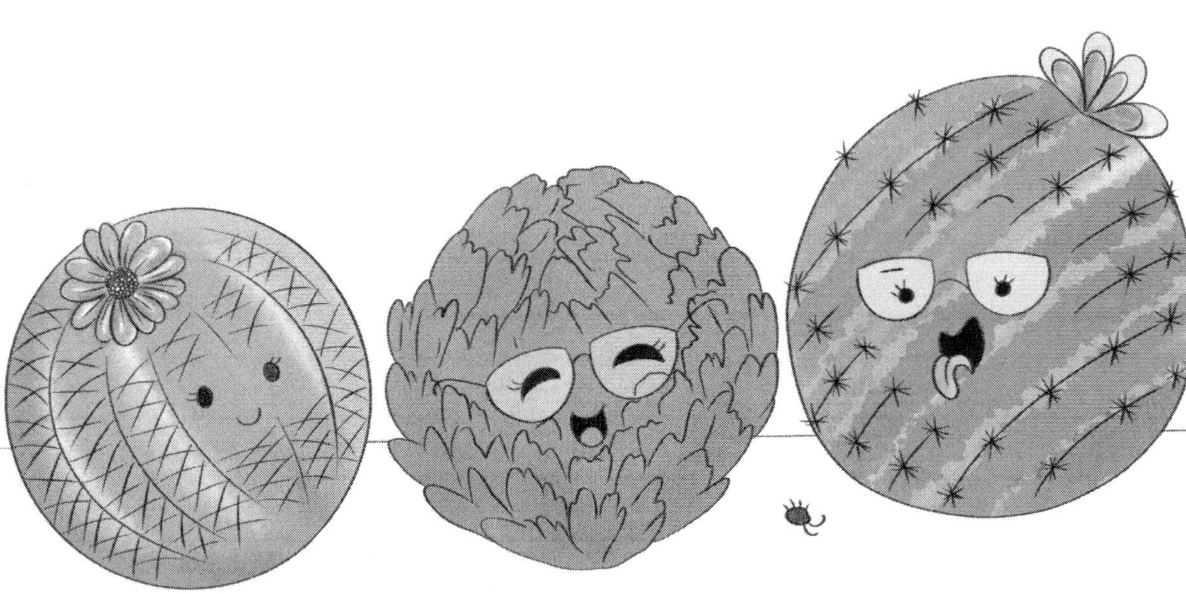

Notes

Notes

NOTES

Notes

NOTES

Notes

NOTES

Notes

NOTES

Notes

NOTES

Renewals

Characactus: Bob Moss

Subscription Name:	Sign-Up Date:
Website: ______	Notes:
Cost: ______	
Renewal Cost: ______	
Renewal Date: ______	
Automatic Renewal: Yes No	

PAYMENT:	REMEMBER TO:
Monthly	Cancel
Annually	Autorenewal
Yearly	Update My Info

Subscription Name:	Sign-Up Date:
Website: ______	Notes:
Cost: ______	
Renewal Cost: ______	
Renewal Date: ______	
Automatic Renewal: Yes No	

PAYMENT:	REMEMBER TO:
Monthly	Cancel
Annually	Autorenewal
Yearly	Update My Info

Subscription Name: | Sign-Up Date:

Website: ______________________

Cost: ______________________

Renewal Cost: ______________________

Renewal Date: ______________________

Automatic Renewal: Yes No

PAYMENT:	REMEMBER TO:
Monthly	Cancel
Annually	Autorenewal
Yearly	Update My Info

Notes: ______________________

____

____

____

____

____

____

____

Subscription Name: | Sign-Up Date:

Website: ______________________

Cost: ______________________

Renewal Cost: ______________________

Renewal Date: ______________________

Automatic Renewal: Yes No

PAYMENT:	REMEMBER TO:
Monthly	Cancel
Annually	Autorenewal
Yearly	Update My Info

Notes: ______________________

____

____

____

____

____

____

____

Subscription Name: Sign-Up Date:

Website: ______________________

Cost: ______________________

Renewal Cost: ______________________

Renewal Date: ______________________

Automatic Renewal: Yes No

PAYMENT:	REMEMBER TO:
Monthly	Cancel
Annually	Autorenewal
Yearly	Update My Info

Notes: ______________________

____

____

____

____

____

____

____

Subscription Name: Sign-Up Date:

Website: ______________________

Cost: ______________________

Renewal Cost: ______________________

Renewal Date: ______________________

Automatic Renewal: Yes No

PAYMENT:	REMEMBER TO:
Monthly	Cancel
Annually	Autorenewal
Yearly	Update My Info

Notes: ______________________

____

____

____

____

____

____

____

Subscription Name: Sign-Up Date:

Website: ______________________

Cost: ______________________

Renewal Cost: ______________________

Renewal Date: ______________________

Automatic Renewal: Yes No

Notes: ______________________

PAYMENT: REMEMBER TO:

Monthly Cancel

Annually Autorenewal

Yearly Update My Info

Subscription Name: Sign-Up Date:

Website: ______________________

Cost: ______________________

Renewal Cost: ______________________

Renewal Date: ______________________

Automatic Renewal: Yes No

Notes: ______________________

PAYMENT: REMEMBER TO:

Monthly Cancel

Annually Autorenewal

Yearly Update My Info

Subscription Name: Sign-Up Date:

Website: ______________________

Cost: ______________________

Renewal Cost: ______________________

Renewal Date: ______________________

Automatic Renewal: Yes No

PAYMENT:	REMEMBER TO:
Monthly	Cancel
Annually	Autorenewal
Yearly	Update My Info

Notes:

Subscription Name: Sign-Up Date:

Website: ______________________

Cost: ______________________

Renewal Cost: ______________________

Renewal Date: ______________________

Automatic Renewal: Yes No

PAYMENT:	REMEMBER TO:
Monthly	Cancel
Annually	Autorenewal
Yearly	Update My Info

Notes:

Subscription Name: Sign-Up Date:

Website: ______________________

Cost: ______________________

Renewal Cost: ______________________

Renewal Date: ______________________

Automatic Renewal: Yes No

Notes: ______________________

PAYMENT: REMEMBER TO:

PAYMENT:	REMEMBER TO:
Monthly	Cancel
Annually	Autorenewal
Yearly	Update My Info

Subscription Name: Sign-Up Date:

Website: ______________________

Cost: ______________________

Renewal Cost: ______________________

Renewal Date: ______________________

Automatic Renewal: Yes No

Notes: ______________________

PAYMENT:	REMEMBER TO:
Monthly	Cancel
Annually	Autorenewal
Yearly	Update My Info

RENEWALS

Subscription Name: Sign-Up Date:

Website: ______________________

Cost: ______________________

Renewal Cost: ______________________

Renewal Date: ______________________

Automatic Renewal: Yes No

PAYMENT:	REMEMBER TO:
Monthly	Cancel
Annually	Autorenewal
Yearly	Update My Info

Notes: ______________________

Subscription Name: Sign-Up Date:

Website: ______________________

Cost: ______________________

Renewal Cost: ______________________

Renewal Date: ______________________

Automatic Renewal: Yes No

PAYMENT:	REMEMBER TO:
Monthly	Cancel
Annually	Autorenewal
Yearly	Update My Info

Notes: ______________________

Subscription Name: Sign-Up Date:

Website: ______________________

Cost: ______________________

Renewal Cost: ______________________

Renewal Date: ______________________

Automatic Renewal: Yes No

Notes: ______________________

PAYMENT: REMEMBER TO:

Monthly Cancel
Annually Autorenewal
Yearly Update My Info

Subscription Name: Sign-Up Date:

Website: ______________________

Cost: ______________________

Renewal Cost: ______________________

Renewal Date: ______________________

Automatic Renewal: Yes No

Notes: ______________________

PAYMENT: REMEMBER TO:

Monthly Cancel
Annually Autorenewal
Yearly Update My Info

Subscription Name: Sign-Up Date:

Website: ______________________

Cost: ______________________

Renewal Cost: ______________________

Renewal Date: ______________________

Automatic Renewal: Yes No

Notes: ______________________

PAYMENT:	REMEMBER TO:
Monthly	Cancel
Annually	Autorenewal
Yearly	Update My Info

Subscription Name: Sign-Up Date:

Website: ______________________

Cost: ______________________

Renewal Cost: ______________________

Renewal Date: ______________________

Automatic Renewal: Yes No

Notes: ______________________

PAYMENT:	REMEMBER TO:
Monthly	Cancel
Annually	Autorenewal
Yearly	Update My Info

Subscription Name: Sign-Up Date:

Website: ______________________

Cost: ______________________

Renewal Cost: ______________________

Renewal Date: ______________________

Automatic Renewal: Yes No

Notes: ______________________

PAYMENT:	REMEMBER TO:
Monthly	Cancel
Annually	Autorenewal
Yearly	Update My Info

Subscription Name: Sign-Up Date:

Website: ______________________

Cost: ______________________

Renewal Cost: ______________________

Renewal Date: ______________________

Automatic Renewal: Yes No

Notes: ______________________

PAYMENT:	REMEMBER TO:
Monthly	Cancel
Annually	Autorenewal
Yearly	Update My Info

Subscription Name: Sign-Up Date:

Website: ______________________

Cost: ______________________

Renewal Cost: ______________________

Renewal Date: ______________________

Automatic Renewal: Yes No

Notes:

PAYMENT:	REMEMBER TO:
Monthly	Cancel
Annually	Autorenewal
Yearly	Update My Info

Subscription Name: Sign-Up Date:

Website: ______________________

Cost: ______________________

Renewal Cost: ______________________

Renewal Date: ______________________

Automatic Renewal: Yes No

Notes:

PAYMENT:	REMEMBER TO:
Monthly	Cancel
Annually	Autorenewal
Yearly	Update My Info

Subscription Name: Sign-Up Date:

Website: ______________________

Cost: ______________________

Renewal Cost: ______________________

Renewal Date: ______________________

Automatic Renewal: Yes No

Notes:

PAYMENT:	REMEMBER TO:
Monthly	Cancel
Annually	Autorenewal
Yearly	Update My Info

Subscription Name: Sign-Up Date:

Website: ______________________

Cost: ______________________

Renewal Cost: ______________________

Renewal Date: ______________________

Automatic Renewal: Yes No

Notes:

PAYMENT:	REMEMBER TO:
Monthly	Cancel
Annually	Autorenewal
Yearly	Update My Info

Subscription Name: Sign-Up Date:

Website: ______

Cost: ______

Renewal Cost: ______

Renewal Date: ______

Automatic Renewal: Yes No

PAYMENT:	REMEMBER TO:
Monthly	Cancel
Annually	Autorenewal
Yearly	Update My Info

Notes: ______

Subscription Name: Sign-Up Date:

Website: ______

Cost: ______

Renewal Cost: ______

Renewal Date: ______

Automatic Renewal: Yes No

PAYMENT:	REMEMBER TO:
Monthly	Cancel
Annually	Autorenewal
Yearly	Update My Info

Notes: ______

Subscription Name: Sign-Up Date:

Website: ______________________

Cost: ______________________

Renewal Cost: ______________________

Renewal Date: ______________________

Automatic Renewal: Yes No

PAYMENT: REMEMBER TO:

PAYMENT	REMEMBER TO
Monthly	Cancel
Annually	Autorenewal
Yearly	Update My Info

Notes: ______________________

____

____

____

____

____

____

____

Subscription Name: Sign-Up Date:

Website: ______________________

Cost: ______________________

Renewal Cost: ______________________

Renewal Date: ______________________

Automatic Renewal: Yes No

PAYMENT: REMEMBER TO:

PAYMENT	REMEMBER TO
Monthly	Cancel
Annually	Autorenewal
Yearly	Update My Info

Notes: ______________________

____

____

____

____

____

____

____

Subscription Name: Sign-Up Date:

Website: ____________

Cost: ____________

Renewal Cost: ____________

Renewal Date: ____________

Automatic Renewal: Yes No

PAYMENT:	REMEMBER TO:
Monthly	Cancel
Annually	Autorenewal
Yearly	Update My Info

Notes: ____________

Subscription Name: Sign-Up Date:

Website: ____________

Cost: ____________

Renewal Cost: ____________

Renewal Date: ____________

Automatic Renewal: Yes No

PAYMENT:	REMEMBER TO:
Monthly	Cancel
Annually	Autorenewal
Yearly	Update My Info

Notes: ____________

RENEWALS

Subscription Name: Sign-Up Date:

Website: ______________________

Cost: ______________________

Renewal Cost: ______________________

Renewal Date: ______________________

Automatic Renewal: Yes No

PAYMENT:	REMEMBER TO:
Monthly	Cancel
Annually	Autorenewal
Yearly	Update My Info

Notes:

____

Subscription Name: Sign-Up Date:

Website: ______________________

Cost: ______________________

Renewal Cost: ______________________

Renewal Date: ______________________

Automatic Renewal: Yes No

PAYMENT:	REMEMBER TO:
Monthly	Cancel
Annually	Autorenewal
Yearly	Update My Info

Notes:

____

Subscription Name: Sign-Up Date:

Website: ____________________

Cost: ____________________

Renewal Cost: ____________________

Renewal Date: ____________________

Automatic Renewal: Yes No

PAYMENT:	REMEMBER TO:
Monthly	Cancel
Annually	Autorenewal
Yearly	Update My Info

Notes: ____________________

Subscription Name: Sign-Up Date:

Website: ____________________

Cost: ____________________

Renewal Cost: ____________________

Renewal Date: ____________________

Automatic Renewal: Yes No

PAYMENT:	REMEMBER TO:
Monthly	Cancel
Annually	Autorenewal
Yearly	Update My Info

Notes: ____________________

RENEWALS

Contacts

Characactus: Sugzorro Cactus

A

B

C

Name: ______________________

Phone Number: ______________________

Email: ______________________

Website: ______________________

Name: ______________________

Phone Number: ______________________

Email: ______________________

Website: ______________________

Name: ______________________

Phone Number: ______________________

Email: ______________________

Website: ______________________

A
B
C

Name: ______________________________

Phone Number: ______________________________

Email: ______________________________

Website: ______________________________

Name: ______________________________

Phone Number: ______________________________

Email: ______________________________

Website: ______________________________

Name: ______________________________

Phone Number: ______________________________

Email: ______________________________

Website: ______________________________

A
B
C

Name: ______________________________

Phone Number: ______________________________

Email: ______________________________

Website: ______________________________

Name: ______________________________

Phone Number: ______________________________

Email: ______________________________

Website: ______________________________

Name: ______________________________

Phone Number: ______________________________

Email: ______________________________

Website: ______________________________

A

B

C

Name:

Phone Number:

Email:

Website:

Name:

Phone Number:

Email:

Website:

Name:

Phone Number:

Email:

Website:

D
E
F

Name: ______________________________

Phone Number: ______________________________

Email: ______________________________

Website: ______________________________

Name: ______________________________

Phone Number: ______________________________

Email: ______________________________

Website: ______________________________

Name: ______________________________

Phone Number: ______________________________

Email: ______________________________

Website: ______________________________

Name: ______________________________

Phone Number: ______________________________

Email: ______________________________

Website: ______________________________

Name: ______________________________

Phone Number: ______________________________

Email: ______________________________

Website: ______________________________

Name: ______________________________

Phone Number: ______________________________

Email: ______________________________

Website: ______________________________

D E F

D
E
F

Name:

Phone Number:

Email:

Website:

Name:

Phone Number:

Email:

Website:

Name:

Phone Number:

Email:

Website:

Name:

Phone Number:

Email:

Website:

Name:

Phone Number:

Email:

Website:

Name:

Phone Number:

Email:

Website:

D

E

F

Name:

Phone Number:

Email:

Website:

G

H

I

Name:

Phone Number:

Email:

Website:

Name:

Phone Number:

Email:

Website:

Name: ________________________________

Phone Number: ____________________________

Email: ________________________________

Website: ______________________________

Name: ________________________________

Phone Number: ____________________________

Email: ________________________________

Website: ______________________________

Name: ________________________________

Phone Number: ____________________________

Email: ________________________________

Website: ______________________________

G
H
I

Name: ______________________________

Phone Number: ______________________________

Email: ______________________________

Website: ______________________________

Name: ______________________________

Phone Number: ______________________________

Email: ______________________________

Website: ______________________________

Name: ______________________________

Phone Number: ______________________________

Email: ______________________________

Website: ______________________________

Name:

Phone Number:

Email:

Website:

Name:

Phone Number:

Email:

Website:

Name:

Phone Number:

Email:

Website:

G
H
I

Name:

Phone Number:

Email:

Website:

Name:

Phone Number:

Email:

Website:

J
K
L

Name:

Phone Number:

Email:

Website:

Name: ____

Phone Number: ________________________________

Email: ____

Website: ______________________________________

Name: ____

Phone Number: ________________________________

Email: ____

Website: ______________________________________

Name: ____

Phone Number: ________________________________

Email: ____

Website: ______________________________________

J

K

L

Name:

Phone Number:

Email:

Website:

Name:

Phone Number:

Email:

Website:

J

K

L

Name:

Phone Number:

Email:

Website:

Name:

Phone Number:

Email:

Website:

Name:

Phone Number:

Email:

Website:

Name:

Phone Number:

Email:

Website:

J

K

L

Name: ______________________

Phone Number: ______________________

Email: ______________________

Website: ______________________

Name: ______________________

Phone Number: ______________________

Email: ______________________

Website: ______________________

Name: ______________________

Phone Number: ______________________

Email: ______________________

Website: ______________________

Name: ____________________

Phone Number: ____________________

Email: ____________________

Website: ____________________

Name: ____________________

Phone Number: ____________________

Email: ____________________

Website: ____________________

Name: ____________________

Phone Number: ____________________

Email: ____________________

Website: ____________________

M
N
O

Name: ______________________________

Phone Number: ______________________________

Email: ______________________________

Website: ______________________________

Name: ______________________________

Phone Number: ______________________________

Email: ______________________________

Website: ______________________________

M

N

O

Name: ______________________________

Phone Number: ______________________________

Email: ______________________________

Website: ______________________________

Name: ______________________________

Phone Number: ______________________________

Email: ______________________________

Website: ______________________________

Name: ______________________________

Phone Number: ______________________________

Email: ______________________________

Website: ______________________________

Name: ______________________________

Phone Number: ______________________________

Email: ______________________________

Website: ______________________________

M
N
O

Name: ______________________________

Phone Number: ______________________________

Email: ______________________________

Website: ______________________________

Name: ______________________________

Phone Number: ______________________________

Email: ______________________________

Website: ______________________________

Name: ______________________________

Phone Number: ______________________________

Email: ______________________________

Website: ______________________________

P

Q

R

Name: ____________________

Phone Number: ____________________

Email: ____________________

Website: ____________________

Name: ____________________

Phone Number: ____________________

Email: ____________________

Website: ____________________

Name: ____________________

Phone Number: ____________________

Email: ____________________

Website: ____________________

P

Q

R

Name: ______________________________

Phone Number: ______________________________

Email: ______________________________

Website: ______________________________

Name: ______________________________

Phone Number: ______________________________

Email: ______________________________

Website: ______________________________

Name: ______________________________

Phone Number: ______________________________

Email: ______________________________

Website: ______________________________

Name: ______________________________

Phone Number: ______________________________

Email: ______________________________

Website: ______________________________

Name: ______________________________

Phone Number: ______________________________

Email: ______________________________

Website: ______________________________

Name: ______________________________

Phone Number: ______________________________

Email: ______________________________

Website: ______________________________

Name: ____________________

Phone Number: ____________________

Email: ____________________

Website: ____________________

Name: ____________________

Phone Number: ____________________

Email: ____________________

Website: ____________________

Name: ____________________

Phone Number: ____________________

Email: ____________________

Website: ____________________

Name: ______________________________

Phone Number: ______________________________

Email: ______________________________

Website: ______________________________

Name: ______________________________

Phone Number: ______________________________

Email: ______________________________

Website: ______________________________

Name: ______________________________

Phone Number: ______________________________

Email: ______________________________

Website: ______________________________

S
T
U

S
T
U

Name: ______________________________

Phone Number: ______________________________

Email: ______________________________

Website: ______________________________

Name: ______________________________

Phone Number: ______________________________

Email: ______________________________

Website: ______________________________

Name: ______________________________

Phone Number: ______________________________

Email: ______________________________

Website: ______________________________

S
T
U

Name: ___

Phone Number: ___

Email: ___

Website: ___

Name: ___

Phone Number: ___

Email: ___

Website: ___

Name: ___

Phone Number: ___

Email: ___

Website: ___

V
W
X
Y
Z

Name: ____________________

Phone Number: ____________________

Email: ____________________

Website: ____________________

Name: ____________________

Phone Number: ____________________

Email: ____________________

Website: ____________________

Name: ____________________

Phone Number: ____________________

Email: ____________________

Website: ____________________

Name:

Phone Number:

Email:

Website:

Name:

Phone Number:

Email:

Website:

Name:

Phone Number:

Email:

Website:

V

W

X

Y

Z

V
W
X
Y
Z

Name: ____________________

Phone Number: ____________________

Email: ____________________

Website: ____________________

Name: ____________________

Phone Number: ____________________

Email: ____________________

Website: ____________________

Name: ____________________

Phone Number: ____________________

Email: ____________________

Website: ____________________

V

W

X

Y

Z

Name: __________

Phone Number: __________

Email: __________

Website: __________

Name: __________

Phone Number: __________

Email: __________

Website: __________

Name: __________

Phone Number: __________

Email: __________

Website: __________

Software Keys

Characactus: Three Scrooges

Software: ____________________

Key: ____________________

Location of Purchase: ____________________

Date of Purchase: ____________________

Software: ____________________

Key: ____________________

Location of Purchase: ____________________

Date of Purchase: ____________________

Software: ____________________

Key: ____________________

Location of Purchase: ____________________

Date of Purchase: ____________________

Software: ____________________

Key: ____________________

Location of Purchase: ____________________

Date of Purchase: ____________________

Software: ____________________

Key: ____________________

Location of Purchase: ____________________

Date of Purchase: ____________________

Software: ____________________

Key: ____________________

Location of Purchase: ____________________

Date of Purchase: ____________________

Software: ______

Key: ______

Location of Purchase: ______

Date of Purchase: ______

Software: ______

Key: ______

Location of Purchase: ______

Date of Purchase: ______

Software: ______

Key: ______

Location of Purchase: ______

Date of Purchase: ______

Software: ______________________________

Key: ______________________________

Location of Purchase: ______________________________

Date of Purchase: ______________________________

Software: ______________________________

Key: ______________________________

Location of Purchase: ______________________________

Date of Purchase: ______________________________

Software: ______________________________

Key: ______________________________

Location of Purchase: ______________________________

Date of Purchase: ______________________________

Characactus: Elvis Prickley

Characactus: Moon Cactus Sonata

Quick Tip

For every password written, insert one incorrect letter or digit in one or two of the boxes. Then use the note section next to the password to remind yourself which box holds the wrong number. For example, there are 13 boxes. If you put the wrong letter in box eight. In your note section, write eight. Then you will know which box to leave out of the password when you use it. Another idea is to make a bookmark that fits over the password boxes. Then notch out some spaces to cover some of the boxes and fill the correct password in the boxes that are notched out. Add incorrect letters to the leftover boxes. That way, your correct answer will only show if you have the bookmark. Just don't lose the bookmarker, or you'll lose your passwords too. Does this sound too complicated? Then come up with your own code or system, just remember, whatever method you use, make sure you use it consistently through the book, or you'll confuse yourself and forget all your passwords.*

P.S. Don't forget to cut out this page so that if you have the bad luck of someone finding your book, they won't understand why all the passwords are coming out wrong, and hopefully, by the time they have cracked your code you might have had a chance to change all of them.

*I am not responsible for you forgetting your passwords. It's hard enough to remember my own. That's why I made this book.

I hope you have enjoyed my creation. Please leave an online review and let me know what you thought of it and if it helped you. 😄

Hello!

Were you expecting something else? Maybe, a book about cactus, perhaps? Don't look so confused. If this book tricked you, then it can fool others, too!

10 (Not So) Interesting Facts About Cactus (That I May Or May Not Have Made Up) is a password book in camouflage. It has been disguised and designed to fit in with most other books on a bookshelf, yet inside, you can organize all of your passwords, contacts, notes, and online subscriptions (along with their renewal dates). There are fun characactus, well, just because I felt like it. Why does a password book have to be boring? There really are ten cactus facts (that I may or may not have made up). This is one time, you should hope that the people who are searching around for your password keeper, judge a book by its cover and end up leaving your book where it belongs, safely on your shelf.

I hope this book helps you spend a little less time trying to figure out where you put that little piece of paper, that had that one password that you really need but can't find, and more time doing things you'd rather be doing, like drawing characactus.

-Jessica R. Herrera

Made in the USA
Monee, IL
05 November 2026

67816254R00111